ADVERTISING A TO Z
FEATURING THE
BLUE WILLOW PATTERN

HELSA MORGAN BOOKS

6 SMYTH PLACE, HAMILTON 3200

NEW ZEALAND

FIRST EDITION

PUBLISHED IN NEW ZEALAND IN 2013

A CIP CATALOGUE RECORD FOR THIS BOOK IS AVAILABLE FROM

THE NATIONAL LIBRARY OF NEW ZEALAND

ISBN 978-0-473-24374-6

INTRODUCTION

In 1993 when I was newly married to my wife Kathy, she introduced me to her Blue Willow collection, which, even at that time, was quite extensive. Living in Australia then, like most collectors we spent many a weekend trawling markets and antique shops searching for new additions to her collection. I say her collection, because at that time I was merely a supportive husband assisting his wife with her collecting passion.

Fast forward to March 1999, in a Sydney antique shop the owner told us about a Willow collecting group in the USA called International Willow Collectors (www.Willowcollectors.org) and that they had an annual convention. Luckily for my wife we were connected to the internet and after some searching she found the club details and yes, there was a convention coming up in July, that year in Richmond, Virginia. We quickly joined the club and booked our trip to Richmond. Prior to the Richmond convention, my thoughts about Willow, were just that of a supportive husband, Richmond changed that. My pre convention thoughts were that this would be a one off trip and that the convention for me would be a boring affair, at least Kathy would be happy. In short we both had such a great time, that by the end of the convention I was already planning our trip to the next annual convention. It was at that convention that I decided to start my own personal Willow collection specialising in advertising pieces. To date (2013), we have attended each annual convention, not only have we collected some fine Willow pieces, we have also made many great friends.

The legend of the Blue Willow pattern is well known and has been documented by many learned writers such as Connie Rogers. I do not profess to be an expert in the intracies and variations quite often seen in the pattern, instead I have just enjoyed searching for advertising which uses the Willow pattern. My collection has become extensive and ranges from free media pieces found in newspapers to antique pieces. In this publication I have catalogued all of the advertising pieces in (mostly) alphabetical order. Where possible I have tried to add some relevant background information to each piece. I would like to thank my wife Kathy who helped me put this publication together. Additionally I would like to thank Ernie Norris, Jeff Siptak, Don LaFont, Harry Hall, Brenda Nottingham and members of International Willow Collectors who provided additional pieces and information for this publication.

The exact origins and who made the first piece of china with the Willow pattern adorning it are still debated by historians of the pattern. I am safe in saying however that in general terms, the pattern originated out of England in the mid to late eighteenth century.

With its birthplace in England, china wares with the Willow pattern soon populated many parts of the world. The popularity of the pattern saw many manufacturers of china use the pattern for their wares and in doing so, they quite often created their own variation of the pattern. Over the years the Willow pattern has become perhaps the most recognised pattern in the world, a pattern that has a legend, history and universal acceptance. It is qualities like these, that advertisers and marketing departments like to associate their products and services with. Therefore it is no surprise that the "Willow pattern brand" has over the past 200 years been used to promote a vast array of products and services. In this book you will see that the pattern has been associated with airlines, beverages, chocolates, cigarettes, souvenirs, restaurants to name a few.

Hugh Sykes

ADLAMS

From what I have been able to find out, Adlams was a small dairy shop in Glastonbury, England. This small waxed carton most likely made in the 1930's would have been used for cream and possibly ice cream.

AIR NEW ZEALAND

Pair of tip trays made by Noritake for Air New Zealand. These trays were used in the First Class cabins of international Air New Zealand flights in the 1960's. The pieces were found individually at markets around Auckland, New Zealand

ANSETT AUSTRALIA

Ansett Australia was a major domestic Australian airline which in the late 1990's commenced flights to international destinations. One of these destinations was Shanghai, China and to advertise this Ansett produced a poster for travel agents to display. The doves in the poster have been replaced by an Ansett plane. Ansett closed for business in 2001. This poster was given to the writer by a Sydney travel agency.

THE ANTIQUARY

Small enamel tray, about 15 cm/6 inches in length. It is a piece advertising "The Antiquary Old Scotch Whisky" with the quote "At last I have found it" The tray features a border that is found on many Willow pattern plates. This piece originates from the USA and was made in the 1860's.

ARDATH CIGARETTES

Ardath was a popular independent brand of cigarettes in Britain up until the late 1940's when the company was taken over by British American Tobacco. This tip tray was likely produced in the 1950's for the British market. The Ardath brand is no longer seen in Britain, however the brand name is still used across several Asian countries.

ARDEN HOTEL

Below are a pair of butter pat dishes made for the Arden Hotel. These pieces in my view are made in England and were most likely part of a wider set of Willow pattern restaurant ware. My research suggests that these were made for the Arden Hotel which is in Stratford Upon Avon, England.

BAGSLATE BRITISH SCHOOL

To mark the opening of Bagslate British School in 1868, these commemorative pieces were made. The school was located in Rochdale, a town close to Manchester, England.

BAU AU LAC

There are many establishments that have used china with the Willow pattern for everyday use. More often their establishment name is displayed in or around the Willow pattern. In this example, Bau Au Lac a prestigious hotel in Zurich, Switzerland has it's name on the reverse along with supplier and manufacturer details.

BAKEWELL CONGREGATIONAL CHURCH

Small Willow pattern plate which has marked in the middle of it "CONGREGATIONAL CHURCH BAKE-WELL" Bakewell is a small town in the English county of Derbyshire. This piece was made in the mid to late 1800's.

BETHSEY DE GARIS

Pictured right, a Willow pattern plate which in the centre shows "Bethsey De Garis 1845". I have not been able to find out anything about Bethsey De Garis, I would suggest that it is a plate made for a person of that name. I am aware that the plates have been seen in the USA and Australia, which adds to the puzzle.

BEAUTY SOAP

Pictured right is a soap wrapper with the words "Willow Beauty Soap" At the time of publication I have to say that I do not know much about this piece, also the quality of the picture is a little hazed. Hopefully a reader will contact me with some information.

Adjacent to this is a soap which has a Willow pattern medallion on it. This soap is made by "Alda's Forever Soap" of Little Rock, Arkansas.

A PRESENT FROM BLACKPOOL

During the 1960's and 70's at many British tourist destinations visitors could purchase a gift where ceramic items would be marked as a "Present from...". In this picture this theme has been adapted as a "Present from Blackpool" a seaside town in England.

BLUE PLATE

An iconic American brand, Blue Plate incorporated a blue Willow plate to market its Blue Plate name. Featured below are two coffee tins, adjacent is the packaging for vanilla essence bottles. Centre are labels from Blue Plate condiment bottles. The history of the Blue Plate brand is extensive and originates from America's dining car history. Dining car restaurants would advertise a "Blue Plate" special where they would use a partitioned grill plate to provide a three course meal at a set and often inexpensive price.

BOOKS

Over the years there have been numerous books both fiction and non fiction that have used the Willow pattern to illustrate the book cover. With the fiction books in most cases, the stories have an oriental theme. Here is a selection. The book titled "Crossing the Blue Willow Bridge" is a true story of an adopted Chinese girl who returns to China.

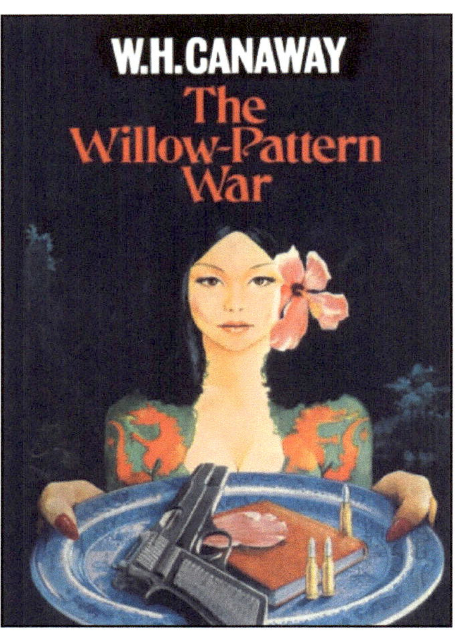

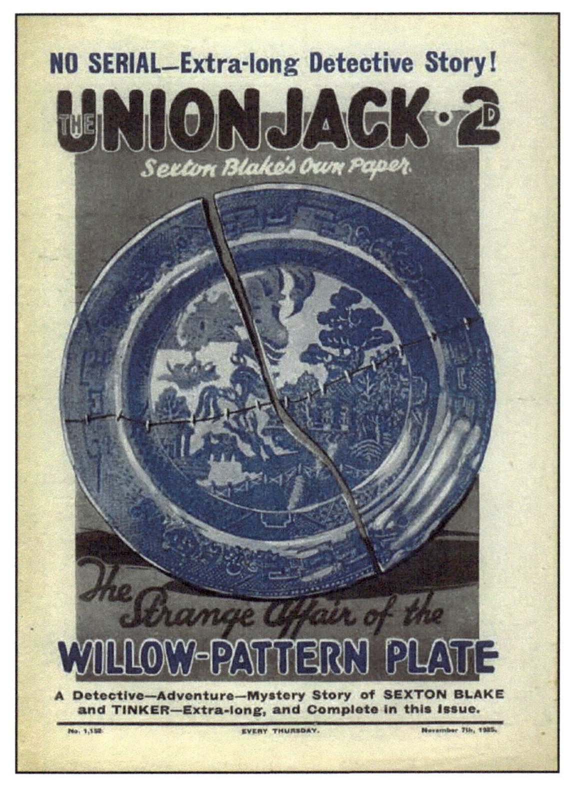

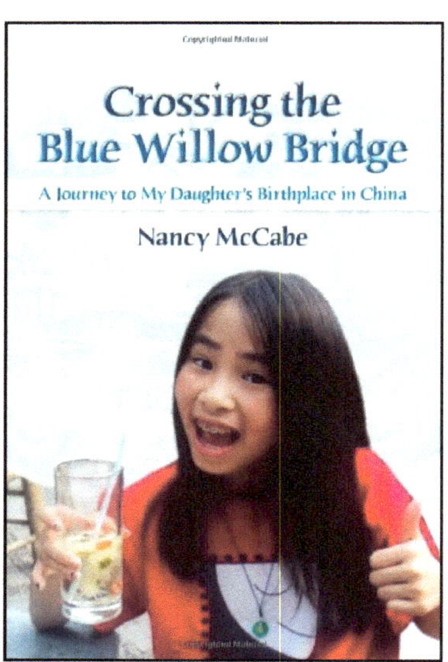

BOOKS

On this page is a selection of non fiction books. To the right Carter's in their 20th anniversary edition for their 2004 antiques price guide used the Willow pattern. The guide does have examples of Willow pattern pieces in it.

Bottom right is a book titled "New Zealand's China Experience" which is a collection of stories about the relationship between New Zealand and China. One story recounts how a breeding group of sheep from New Zealand arrived in Shanghai and then had to be transported by river boat 2,000 miles to their inland destination. Who knows, their wool may have ended up in a Willow pattern jumper.

Below is a book titled "In The Eastern Manner" produced by the Museum of Applied Art & Science (Australia). This book published in 1980 details the growth of Australia's trade relationship with the growing economies of China and Japan.

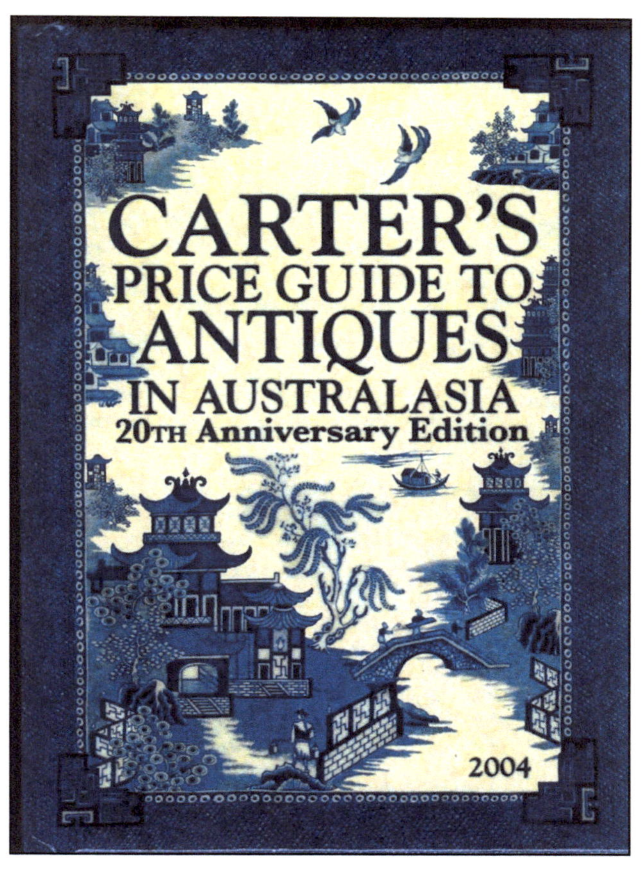

BREESE'S BEE HOVENS CLIP

Pictured bottom left is the front cover of a book published by Breese's Bee of London manufacturers of ladies under garments such as stocking holders and suspender belts known as Hoven's Clip. Inside the book is a rhyme themed on the story of the Willow pattern which leads the reader to a final line which includes the use of "Hoven's Clip". This book was most likely published in the late 1800's.

Of interest is the association that Alfred Breese had with the Willow pattern as pictured to the right from a newspaper dated 1889 he advertises a book on the Willow Pattern Plate and next to this advertisement he advertises his "Hoven's Hose Holder".

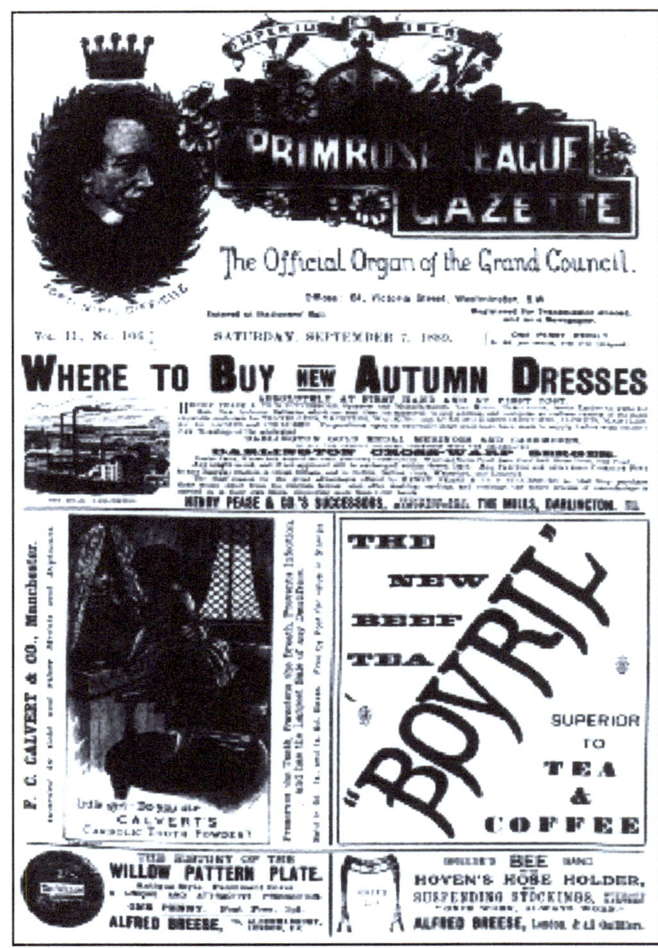

BLUE WILLOW RESTAURANT

Around the world there are many restaurants and eateries that use "Blue Willow" as their establishment name. This menu card and voucher is from the Blue Willow restaurant in Edmonton, Canada.

BRIC A BRAC RAG

Front cover of piano sheet music in the rag time theme titled Bric-a-Brac Rag by Maurice Porcelain, which was published in 1906 by Vinton Music of Boston & New York.

BRIDGE END STORE

Small Willow pattern plate which has marked in the middle of it "BRIDGE END STORE". Store location is probably in the North East of England. This piece was made in the mid to late 1800's.

A PRESENT FROM BRIDGEND

During the 1960's and 70's at many British tourist destinations visitors could purchase a gift where ceramic items would be marked as a "Present from...". In this picture this theme has been adapted as a "Present from Bridgend", a town in Wales.

BURLEIGH WILLOW

Burleigh a major English pottery was established in the mid 1800's by founders William Leigh and Frederick Burgess. Following their deaths, the business continued under the control of their sons Edmund Leigh and Richard Burgess. In 1905 Edmund Leigh asked Thomas Wood Heath to represent Burgess & Leigh in Australia. The name of Wood Heath represented Burgess & Leigh "Burleigh" in Australia until 2002 when the business closed. At one time the business was located in "Burleigh House" 232 Clarence Street, Sydney. This piece was probably used by their sales people to advertise the location of their Sydney and Melbourne stores.

BUSCH'S

Set of 4 pieces with the Willow pattern set in brown. The name "Busch's" is a chain of supermarkets in the mid states of the USA. These pieces were most likely produced in the 1980's.

BUTTER DISHES (WOODEN SURROUND)

As a tourist souvenir, visitors to many British seaside towns (and other tourist destinations) could as a memento purchase a "butter dish" encased in a wooden surround. Carved in the surround would be the name of the town. All the examples featured here are from seaside towns. The dishes all measure 15cm/6 inches across (not including surround) and were made in the 1920 -30s.

CANADIAN PACIFIC

Advertisement for Canadian Pacific to promote their "Orient" passenger rail service across Canada from east coast locations to the west coast. Whilst the Canadian Pacific railroad company exists today, its passenger services were taken over by Via Rail in the 1980's with the Canadian Pacific Orient route taken over in 1986. This print was most likely produced in the 1970's and used by Travel Agents as a promotional flyer, in this case by travel agency Thomas Cook.

CADBURY'S CUP CHOCOLATE

Printed advertisement for Cadbury's drinking chocolate. Cadbury's is a British company which is well known for it's chocolate and confectionary products. The company has since merged with Schweppes, now known as Cadbury Schweppes. Likely print date of this advertisement, late 1940's to 1950's.

CAMPBELL'S

Colour newspaper advertisement from the Saturday Evening Post for Campbell's Cream of Chicken Soup. In this advertisement, Campbell's have associated their soup as having old fashioned qualities drawn from an old farmhouse kitchen. A Willow pattern coupe and underplate have been used to display the soup. Campbell's are an iconic American brand and are a global company. This advertisement would have featured in the 1940's and 1950's .

CAPE ANN (USA)

Blue Willow pattern poster which was designed to feature many of the local coastal attractions of Cape Ann, a fishing town located on the North East coast of the USA.

CAPE COD MASS.

Souvenir plate which has for it's feature a map of the Cape Cod region. Surrounding the central feature is a traditional border design seen on many blue Willow pattern plates.

C.B.S. SCHOOL

At the time of writing this book, I have not been able find any information about C.B.S. School. What I can say is that these pieces in a Willow pattern are similar to the Croft Street Wesleyan School piece shown in this book which have a date of 1880. On this premise I would guess that C.B.S. was a Sunday School somewhere in England and these pieces were made to celebrate a milestone in the school's history.

CELESTIAL TEA

Celestial tin tea caddy containing a 1/2 lb. of Pure China Tea. The caddy has a Willow medallion on each of it's outward facing sides. The tea was sold by R. E. Brand & Co Ltd of London.

YE OLDE CHESHIRE CHEESE

Willow patterned plate which is approximately 20cm/8 inches in diameter. The top of the plate has the words "YE OLDE CHESHIRE CHEESE" below these words "WINE OFFICE COURT" and in the middle of these words a cheese with the address 145 Fleet Street. (London)

CHARLIE'S SANDWICH SHOPPE

Charlie's Sandwich Shoppe established in 1927 is an American Diner located in Boston (USA). This piece would have been used to serve soup and chilli.

CHINA GIRL

Restaurant ware plate featuring the Willow pattern in red. Location of "China Girl" restaurant is unknown, however the piece was obtained in the USA.

CHINS

Restaurant ware plate featuring the Willow pattern in red. Location of "Chins" restaurant is unknown, however the piece was obtained in the USA.

CHINA MOON

Cover for the musical publication "China Moon". The Willow pattern has been used as a background to depict a general theme of this musical which was staged in London in the 1950's.

THE CHINA HOUSE

Paper placemat made for "The China House" restaurant.

CHRISTMAS CARDS

Pictured on this page are a selection of Christmas Cards which feature the Willow pattern. Collectors of cards would I am sure be able to place and dates these cards.

My guess and based on the Willow pattern displayed on these cards, are that they date somewhere between the late 1800's to the 1920's.

CHUNG LING SOO

Chung Ling Soo was an American stage magician who was born in April 1861 and died in March 1918 at the age of 56. Chung Ling Soo was the stage name of William Robinson.

Chung Ling Soo who originally started performing under his real name in the USA came to London in 1905 and it was there that he adopted his Chinese name in keeping with his Chinese themed magical show. To the world at large he was known as Chung Ling Soo with only stage crew and fellow magicians knowing that he was not Chinese. One could devote a whole book to the works and life of Chung Ling Soo, indeed books have been written, along with a modern feature length movie. In this book however I am only touching on Chung Ling Soo's use of the Willow pattern plate to promote his show. Chung Ling Soo's most famous illusion was that of catching a bullet shot from a gun, in this act he would catch a bullet in his hands or in some instances between his teeth. The reality was that live bullets identified by the audience were during the act changed for blanks. In March 1918, the act went terribly wrong, with the switch of bullets not occurring which resulted in Chung Ling Soo receiving a fatal bullet to the chest. His death was recorded as an accident. Needless to say his story lives on in keeping with the enduring legend of the Willow pattern plate.

COOPERATIVE SOCIETY

Cooperative Societies were popular in Britain, many of which were established in the mid to late 1800's. The two plates shown immediately below were produced to celebrate the Diamond Jubilee of the respective societies, Gomersal Industrial in 1928 and Gainscross & Foley in 1923 . The plate bottom right was produced in 1929 to mark the Jubilee of the Butt Lane Industrial Cooperative Society. The plates measure 30 cm /12 inches across and show the Willow pattern around the plate border.

Pictured bottom left is a plate which has a centre marking "R & P Co-operative Society" with the phrase " Nothing Without Labour". The style of pattern and wording suggests that this piece was made in the mid to late 1800's.

CRAWFORDS SCOTCH WHISKY

Crawford's Scotch Whisky, also known as A & A Crawford's. This Scottish whisky distiller produced a number of breweriana pieces which would support the sales of their product in bars and restaurants around Britain.

CROFT STREET WESLEYAN SUNDAY SCHOOL

Small Willow patterned plate made for Croft Street Wesleyan Sunday School. The plate adds further detail in that the school is in Preston (England) and has a date of 1880.

CHOYSA TEA

Tea tin from New Zealand which has on it several tea pots, the predominant one has the Willow pattern in brown.

PURE FRESH CREAM

Waxed carton which contained 3.9 fluid ounces of fresh cream. The carton has a height of 10cm/4 inches with a similar opening diameter. The carton has the Willow pattern around it and comes from England. The carton was most likely made in the 1930's.

ALBERTO'S CHURROS

Table menu from restaurant chain "Alberto's who are known for their Spanish Churros (which are a variation of a donut, or is the other way round.)

CUNARD LINE

Pictured here is the front of a restaurant menu card from the Cunard Line passenger ship RMS Lancastria. This menu card was produced in 1928. The Lancastria was launched in 1920 and was able to carry 2,200 persons. Requisitioned by the British government at the start of World War Two, she became a troop carrier. On June 17th 1940 the Lancastria with over 9,000 persons on board was sunk three miles off the coast of France with the loss of 4,000 persons, the worst ever maritime loss of life.

DAVIDSON'S

Davidson's are a producer of fine boutique teas and with their product packaging have used a Willow pattern tea-pot or a cup and saucer as a centre theme.

DONALD FISHER

Advertising tip tray which is very similar in design to tip trays produced by Schweppes. Donald Fisher's Whisky was a boutique whisky producer in Edinburgh, Scotland which has since been taken over by a larger producer. This piece was probably made in the 1930's. It is interesting to take a look at the makers mark, which is in itself an advertisement for the maker of the piece, in this instance "Messrs" Green & Nephew, London, Designers & Manufacturers of Advertising Specialties.

EMPIRE HOTEL

Willow patterned plate marked "Empire Hotel Queenstown" My research suggests that this piece comes from Queenstown on the west coast of Ireland. Queenstown is historically known as a port through which millions of migrants passed en route to New World countries.

EXXON

In 1991 oil company Exxon used aspects of the Willow pattern as a background theme for the cover of their annual report. The picture shows a map of Hong Kong and surrounding Territories.

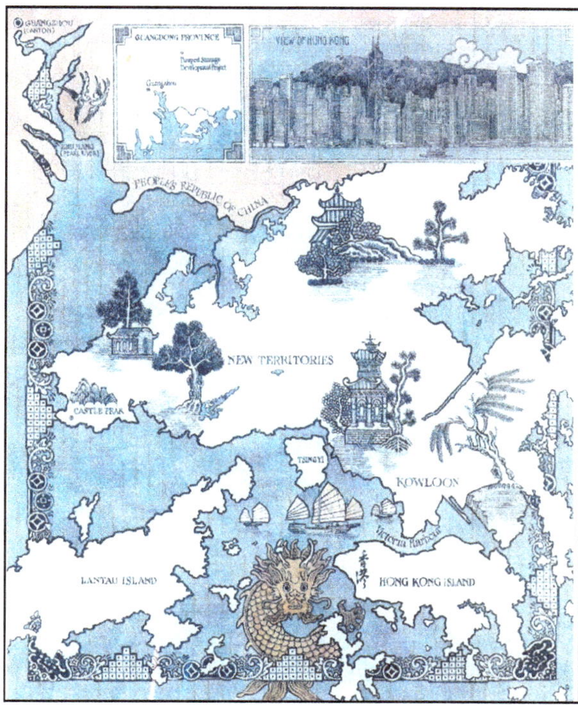

EVERINGHAM THE BUTCHER

Small tureen made for "Everingham The Butcher 1935" who today are still located in the city of Leeds, England.

FAILSWORTH NATIONAL SUNDAY SCHOOL

Small tea pot set in Willow pattern with the words Failsworth National Sunday School 1856. Failsworth is a suburb of Manchester, England, the school mentioned was built in 1837 by the Church of England with support from the Government and the National Society. It was one of the first "National" schools to operate as a Sunday and weekday school. The school which was eventually absorbed into the modern education system closed in 1963. My guess is that whilst the school officially opened in 1837, it was probably opened in 1836, hence this piece celebrates 20 years.

FAIRY COCOA

Circular card which advertises Fairy Cocoa. The reverse of the card has information about the product and supplier Schweitzer's Cocoatina Co of 143 York Road, London, England. The card also mentions that purchasers should collect coupons to redeem for "Willow Pattern China of English make".

FLAV—O—RICH INC

Flav - O - Rich from Louisville, Kentucky used Willow pattern china to advertise their ice cream. The tub which holds a half gallon of ice cream was made in 2001.

TOM FILLERY'S

Pictured below a tin containing three and half ounces of assorted toffee which were made for Canadian company Walter E Jacques & Sons Ltd of Hamilton. The toffees are made by Tom Fillery's of England. This tin made in England was most likely produced in the 1960's and becomes an advertising piece by virtue of the sticker placed on it.

FLINT CO

Pictured here is a cup which has its advertising message on the base inside. At the time when this cup was most likely produced in the early part of the 1900's, Flint Co (established 1864) was a major Rhode Island household goods retailer. Customers were able to purchase goods on an installment plan, an advertising message noted in this piece.

FONG'S GARDEN

Restaurant ware piece with a red Willow pattern border with the words "Fong's Garden". At this point in time, that is about as much as I can say about this piece other than to mention that Fong's Garden is most likely the name of a Chinese Restaurant.

FONDA

Fonda are a manufacturer of disposable tableware such as the cups and plates pictured below. These Willow patterned items were available during the 1970's when a carton of 25 cups could be purchased for 41 cents (USA).

FORTUNES

Fortunes are suppliers of tea products such as those shown here. They have used the Willow pattern on their wooden box packaging which contain tea bags.

FAR EAST RESTAURANT

Advertising piece for Far East Restaurant which was probably used as a cup for the drinking of china tea. Whereabouts of the restaurant is unknown, however the cup displays a phone number which with some investigation could be located.

FRY'S CHOCOLATE

J.S. Fry & Sons Ltd were British chocolate and cocoa manufacturers. During the 1930's they produced a collection of cards (similar to cigarette cards). This card is number 12 out of 15 in a series depicting China & Porcelain. The reverse of the card details a brief history of the Willow pattern.

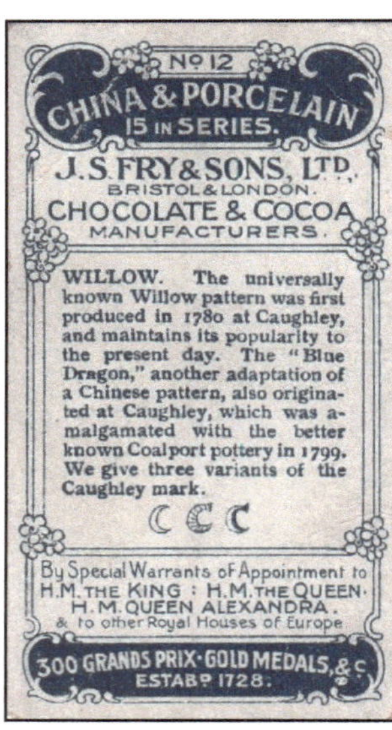

GADD & COX

Gadd & Cox (also known as G & C) paper bag packaging for their "Empire Tips Tea". This packaging contained 1/4 lb. of tea (approx. 120 grams). Such packaging was typical of tea sold in Britain up until the late 1960's.

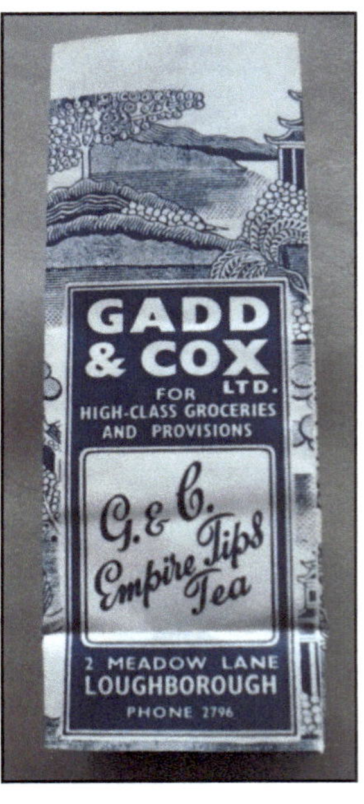

THOMAS GIBSON

Advertising piece which has used the Willow pattern border. This piece was most likely produced in the late 1800's. Thomas Gibson of Southport, a coastal town in the north of England were glass and china dealers and operated from two stores until their closure in the 1960's.

GRAY DUNN

Gray Dunn were a Scottish based biscuit maker that was established in 1853. Over the years, particularly in the first part of the 20th century it produced some very collectable biscuit tins, some having values today of in excess of US$5,000. This tin with the Willow pattern was most likely produced in the 1960's. The company closed in 2001.

JOSEPH GILLOTTS

Joseph Gillotts is a company which has been manufacturing high quality dip pens since 1827. The company is named after it's founder Joseph Gillott. Pictured here is a match box size box made of card that would have contained a gross of ink nibs.

GUINNESS

This plate is perhaps one of the most widely known advertising pieces using the Willow pattern. Instead of running away with the Mandarin's daughter, Chang is seen running away with a Pint of Guinness Beer. Here the Mandarin is shouting "My Goodness My Guinness". This plate was most likely made in the 1950's. Guinness Beer is still widely drunk across all parts of the world.

GLADSTONE

Over the past 20 years the Gladstone Pottery located in Stoke on Trent, England have produced a number of Willow pattern inspired souvenir plates and ornaments for towns and cities across Britain. With the plates, the Willow pattern has been used, but varied to incorporate local attractions.

Plate representing the city of York, the prominent variation is York Abbey replacing the Pagoda

Plate representing the city of London. In this plate the Willow pattern has been extensively modified to show many famous city attractions.

Salt shaker which was made for the English spa town of Droitwich.

Plate representing the city of Lincoln. In this plate, aspects of the Willow pattern have been varied to show Lincoln Cathedral and a World War 2 Lancaster bomber (which were flown from nearby airfields).

GIANNA

Established in 1986 and located in Hong Kong, Gianna Co Ltd are purveyors of gourmet teas which are sourced from China. With this tin tea caddy they have used it to package Jasmine tea, which in turn was sold in the Australian market. The tin was produced in the early 1990's (with the tea contents having a use by date of December 1995).

HANKOW- BATCHELOR

Pair of tins produced by British tea purveyors Hankow—Batchelor who have been trading since 1880. It is most likely that these tins were part of a series, with each tin containing 10 tea bags and having a different blend of tea. Hankow—Batchelor are well known for producing collectible tea tins and my estimate is that these tins were made in the 1980's.

HARRIS & MARSH

Small unassuming Willow pattern dish. As with several pieces in this publication, the story and the history are the words on the reverse. In this case, we can see that this piece was made for Harris & Marsh Pty Ltd of Hobart, which is the capital city of the Australian island state Tasmania. Harris & Marsh were established in 1912 and traded as a large department store until the 1950's. My research suggests that this piece was probably made in the 1920's. The company also produced a set of picture postcards around the same time, which on the reverse detailed blue and white china they had for sale. At the time of publication I have not yet been able to source one of these cards, but will keep looking.

HAMMONDS GUARDS ALE

Hammonds United Breweries was a small British brewer based in Bradford in the county of Yorkshire. Pictured here is a beer mat made of card which advertises their Guards Ale. This ale was one of their stronger bottled beverages. This beer mat was most likely made in the 1950's. The company was taken over in 1960.

HANNAY & DICKSON

This piece a water or beer jug was produced in the 1860s for Hannay & Dickson who operated pubs and wine bars in Manchester, England. This jug was dug out of the ground by a gardener. It was probably discarded as the jug is missing it's handle and has damage to the spout.

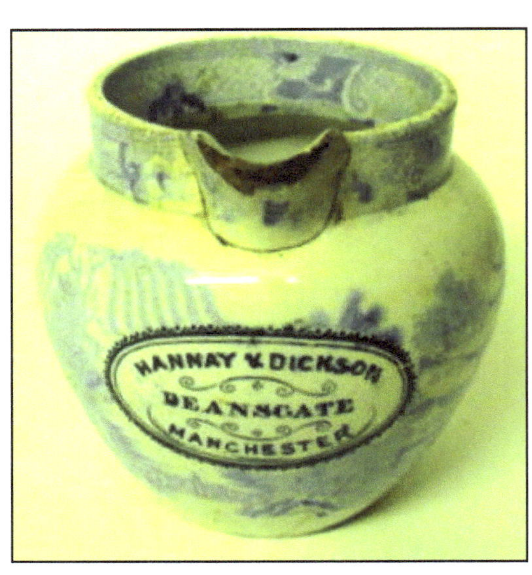

HENRY MORGAN SC LIMITED

Henry Morgan SC Limited is a Canadian department store chain founded by Scotsman Henry Morgan. In 1845 Morgan opened a retail dry goods store in Montreal, later in 1866 his business moved to a department store theme which he expanded across Quebec and Ontario. The business remained in the family until 1960 when it was bought by the Hudson Bay Company. The piece below probably pre dates 1960 and was most likely commissioned by the company as part of a wider Willow pattern set.

HOTEL & RESTAURANT WARE

Pictured on this page are two small Willow pattern dishes that would most likely have been used as butter pats in restaurants and hotels. Both of these pieces have been supplied to the restaurant and hotel trade by suppliers, details of which are marked on the back of each piece. The first piece is supplied by "Cook's Hotel and Restaurant Supply" of New York, who started trading in the 1920's, closing in 1971.

The second piece is supplied by New York china supplier Higgins & Seiter who traded from the 1860's before closing in 1915 when the partnership went bankrupt. Higgins & Seiter were known as quality retailers of fine china which they sourced domestically and from the potteries of England and Europe.

There are other suppliers which I shall endeavor to include in a later publication.

HSBC

HSBC is a global bank which used this advertisement in the Australian paper media to show that clients (exporters) like the Willow pattern were not all the same. The article shows 12 variations of the Willow pattern.

HUNTLEY & PALMER

Huntley & Palmer is a British biscuit manufacturer that was established in 1822. It has a long history of producing biscuit tins for its products. The tins below were most likely produced in the 1970s. The brand name of Huntley & Palmer is still in existence today, though not of the scale seen in the 20th century.

Pictured below, biscuit tin with Willow pattern in red made for Macy's by Huntley & Palmer.

HEALEY CONSERVATIVE CLUB

Trio of pieces which are marked "Healey Conservative Club 1887". The club which is still in existence today is in Manchester, England. By name the club is associated with the British Conservative political party, with profits from this club (of which there are many) being used to support the political activities of the Conservative Party. Originating out of London, the clubs during the mid to late 1800's spread across the rest of the country and these pieces pictured would indicate that Healey Conservative Club was established in 1887.

JAFFEE

Pictured below is an advertisement for Jaffee in the Lady's Home Journal which was published in July 1948. Jaffee a powdered drink was made by the Beech Nut Packaging Company of Canajoharie, New York which was established in 1891. While the brand name of Beech Nut Packaging survives today, ownership of product rights and production has over recent times been sold to various international companies. When produced, Jaffee was known as a caffeine free alternative to coffee and tea as the product was made from blended fruits and cereals. In this picture we see Jaffee served in a Willow patterned cup.

J & G STEWARTS

Adjacent is an ashtray displaying the advertising mark for J & G Stewart's "Finest Old Scotch Whisky". Although the ashtray is unmarked, it is made in England and was produced during the 1930's.

JAMIE STUART

Jamie Stuart a Scottish whisky maker produced during the 1930's this ashtray and water jug to promote their Scotch and Liqueur whiskies.

W KESLAKE

Extensive research by the writer has not yielded any definitive information as to who W Keslake might be. Based on the style of writing, this piece was probably made in the late 1800's. As for W Keslake, my thoughts are that he, William was a ship's captain and this was one of his dining plates. During the 1890's and early 1900's William Keslake commanded the SS Urmston, a ship that sailed between Europe, Australia and New Zealand.

KING

Restaurant ware plate with a variant of the Willow pattern in green. The plate has the word "KING" and would most likely be the name of the restaurant, details of the restaurant are unknown.

KITCHENER CIGARS

Tip tray from Britain, similar in size and design to those made for Schweppes. This piece from the 1920's advertises two brands of Kitchener Cigars being their Red Band and Green Band.

KORDA MENTHA

Korda Mentha are an Australasian accounting firm who have offices across New Zealand and Australia. In 2008 the New Zealand office placed the advertisement below in the New Zealand Herald to show their support for Mahe Drysdale a single skulls rower bound for the 2008 Beijing Olympics (where he got a bronze medal). Mahe is still rowing for New Zealand and competed in the London 2012 Olympics where he won a gold medal.

KYLIN

Kylin produced an extensive range of oriental cooking sauces and soups for the North American retail market. With their labeling, they used the Willow pattern to promote the oriental essence of their products. Pictured below are marketing used and actual product containers.

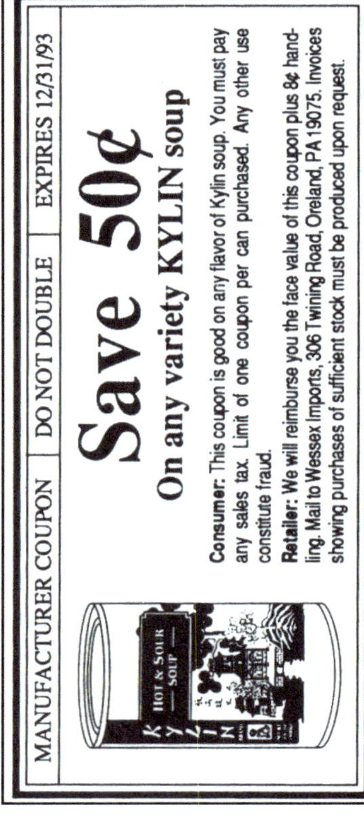

MANUFACTURER COUPON | DO NOT DOUBLE | EXPIRES 12/31/93

Save 50¢
On any variety KYLIN soup

Consumer: This coupon is good on any flavor of Kylin soup. You must pay any sales tax. Limit of one coupon per can purchased. Any other use constitute fraud.

Retailer: We will reimburse you the face value of this coupon plus 8¢ handling. Mail to Wessex Imports, 306 Twining Road, Oreland, PA 19075. Invoices showing purchases of sufficient stock must be produced upon request.

KOW SUN

Restaurant ware plate showing the Willow pattern in red advertising "Kow Sun". The restaurant of this name is not known, though it is most likely a Chinese restaurant as Kow and Sun are known Chinese names.

SOUVENIR OF THE LONE STAR RANCH

Pictured here is a small unassuming Willow pattern jug. On the jug is a sticker which reads "Souvenir Of The Lone Star Ranch". With such a popular name , my thoughts are that this piece comes from the "Lone Star" state of Texas.

SOUVENIR OF
The Lone Star Ranch

C KREJSA

Luster ware plate which has a multi coloured variation of the Willow pattern. The plate carries the words "C Krejsa For Furniture". My research suggests that the "C" is an initial for Charles who as Charles Krejsa was born in 1886 and died in 1968. During his life he operated a furniture store under his own name at 5203 Fleet Avenue, Cleveland, Ohio. I have sighted records showing that the business was operating in 1933, but I have been unable to confirm when it was established (or closed). This plate would of probably been a give-away to business patrons and my estimation is that this plate was probably produced in the 1930's.

ON LOCK SAM

Restaurant ware plate made for Chinese Restaurant "On Lock Sam" which serves diners in Stockton, California. The restaurant was established in 1898.

LARKIN

The Larkin Soap Manufacturing Company of the USA was established in 1875 and came to prominence in Buffalo. In addition to selling premium soap products which it manufactured, the company also sold other premium products such as china. Seeing the success of retailing premium products, the company in 1901 established the Buffalo Pottery to provide quality pottery products for sale. To many Willow collectors, Buffalo Pottery is well known. This picture shows Buffalo Pottery with the Willow pattern marketed under the Larkin Plan and notes the year 1918. Buffalo pieces are marked with their year of manufacture. The Larkin Plan enabled customers to purchase goods on installments.

LAXTON CAMBRIDGE

Pictured below is an English compote which has the words " Laxton Cambridge" This piece dates around the mid to late 1800's and was most likely commissioned by the Laxton family who in the 1800's and for the first half of the 1900's were a prominent Cambridge family. The Laxton's were known for their retailing interests which followed on from their plant and nursery activities. In particular Thomas Laxton was a pioneer in plant science who also provided advice to the scientist Charles Darwin.

PRESENT FROM LLANGOLLEN

Small jug and bowl which has the words "Present from Llangollen". These tourist souvenirs were popular in Britain during the 1960's and 70's". Llangollen is a popular seaside town on the coast of Wales.

LARGE & TOWNLEY

Pictured below is a demitasse cup and saucer in the Willow pattern made by Copeland which would have been produced in the mid to late 1800's. This cup and saucer is fairly typical, however the mark on both pieces in addition to the Copeland mark is Large & Townley (of) Napier. Large & Townley were New Zealand cabinet makers in Napier a coastal North Island town and traded between the years 1867 and 1896.

LUCEYS HOLLYWOOD

Restaurant ware plate showing the "Masons" variation of the Willow pattern in red. Luceys was a Spanish style restaurant located at 5444 Melrose, Windsor (Los Angeles), California. During the 1940's and 50's the restaurant was frequented regularly by the rich and famous. Today the restaurant has gone, with the building now used as an office.

LUTHERAN CHURCH

Pictured below is a 50 year commemorative plate, 1884 to 1934, which was commissioned by St Paul's Evangelical Lutheran Church. In this example the central Willow pattern has been removed and replaced by a picture of the Lutheran Church. A typical Willow pattern border has been retained.

LUTE SONG

Music sheets from the American musical Lute Song. The musical opened on Broadway February 1946 running for 142 performances, closing June 1946. The musical in 1948 also showed in London, which is where these music sheets originate from. The theme of the Lute Song is a love story very similar to the Willow legend, hence the use of the Willow pattern.

LIPTONS TEA

Liptons Tea which today is a global brand owned by Unilever of the USA was founded in 1888 by Scotsman Thomas Lipton. In 1870 Lipton opened a provisions store in Glasgow, Scotland, though prior to this he spent five years working a number of jobs across the USA. His business activities as a store owner were a success and by 1888 his empire had grown to 300 stores. It was at this time he entered the tea trade, dealing directly with plantations so that he could deliver tea to his stores at a cheaper price. This enterprise was a success and Liptons Tea was soon being distributed across Europe and North America. Thomas Lipton was knighted by Queen Victoria and died in 1931 at the age of 83.

Pictured below is a small tea caddy which is impressed on the base "Liptons Tea Largest Sale In The World" Judging by the appearance of the tin and similar tins seen in this book, I would estimate that this tin was most likely made between 1890 and 1910.

A PRESENT FROM MENAI BRIDGE

Small cup and saucer which has the words 'Present From Menai Bridge". The pattern and style of wording is very similar to other tourist souvenirs in this book made for the towns of Blackpool, Llangollen and Bridgend.

Menai Bridge is a British coastal town in North Wales.

MACINTOSH

Macintosh a British manufacturer of toffees was established in the 1890's by Yorkshire man John Macintosh. The company remained in family ownership until 1969 and is now owned by Nestle. This tin was most likely produced in the 1960's and contained a selection of toffees. The tin lid features the Willow pattern, with the tin having a Christmas theme.

MACLENNAN'S

MacLennan's was a British soft drinks company that used to do home deliveries. Each week a lemonade truck would visit local neighborhoods to sell bottled lemonade, and collect returned bottles. This tip tray was likely produced in the 1950's.

MACROBERTSON CHOCOLATES

Pictured right is a chocolate box, made of card produced by MacRobertson's of Melbourne, Australia. This box contained a 1/2 lb. of chocolates known as "The Willow Box of Old Gold Chocolates" The factory that produced Old Gold Chocolates was built in the 1920's and it is said that an Old Gold selection of chocolates was the ultimate gift for lovers of chocolate. This box was likely produced in the 1930's

MacRobertson's officially known as the MacRobertson's Steam Confectionery Works was founded in 1880 by Sir MacPherson Robertson. In 1967 the family business was sold to British confectioners Cadbury (who later became Cadbury Schweppes). The modern day business still operates from a MacRobertson factory and chocolate under the Old Gold name is still sold.

MANCHESTER TAILORING DEPOT

Small ceramic medallion type piece measuring approx. 7 cm/3 inches in diameter dating to the late 1800's. The centre of the piece has the words "Manchester Tailoring Depot Bolton" being a men's tailoring shop. A hole is seen at the top of the piece, this would enable the piece to be attached to a garment.

MILADY'S SHOP

Pictured below are the front and back of an advertising postcard issued by Milady's Shop of the USA a women's apparel retailer. The card provides an offer to customers that if they add to their account or make a purchase of at least $19.95 they will receive a 20—piece dinner set in the Willow pattern. Looking at the card and noting that the dinner set is imported, the dinner set has the Willow pattern favored by Japanese manufacturers.

MITCHELLS & BUTLERS

Mitchells & Butlers today is a significant British company with extensive brewery and leisure interests. This piece was most likely produced when the company was a regional brewery in the British Midlands, being made in the 1950's and advertises the signature beer of the company "Deers Leap". The company is known for supplying beer to the Allied Troops during the Normandy landings during World War 2.

MODERN HOME

Pictured below is a piece of "Old Bleach" linen featuring the Willow pattern. Measuring 20 cm/8 inches square, this piece was a supplement giveaway from "Modern Home" a British magazine in October 1929. The magazine was a monthly publication at the time and sold for sixpence. Readership of the magazine was aimed at the lady of the house who would have been interested in reading light romantic stories and doing home crafts such as needlework and embroidery. My guess is that this piece would have been framed as a picture or used as a template for embroidery.

THE MUTUAL STORE

This unassuming bowl showing the blue Willow pattern was made for "The Mutual Store" Melbourne, Australia which established in 1872 was Melbourne's first department store. The business operated as a cooperative between staff and shareholders until 1961 when it was sold to a private company. The business closed in 1965. The bowls were sold complete with a pudding.

JOHN MORTLOCK

John Mortlock "Mortlocks" were a London merchandiser of fine china. Whilst this piece notes establishment in 1746, the actual year was 1794. Mortlocks were purveyors of fine china and had 3 stores, their last store Portman Square opened in 1873. This piece which measures 5 cm/2 inches across was most likely produced in the late 1800's. In their time Mortlocks were suppliers of china to Queen Victoria. They also got their suppliers to put the Mortlocks mark on china they sold. The Mortlocks china retailing business closed in 1933.

NELSON MOATES

Nelson Moates established in the late 1800's were at the beginning of the 1900's the largest importers of tea into New Zealand, sourced at that time from Ceylon (now known as Sri Lanka). They also sold tea in Australia and America. These tins pictured with the blue Willow pattern are all from the early 1900's. To the right a 1 lb. tin of "Sterling Tea", bottom left a 1lb tin of regular tea and bottom right a 5 lb. tin. All of the tins make mention that the company won medals at the Auckland and Christchurch exhibitions which were held in 1902.

NEWS OF THE WORLD

Pictured below is a coaster which was a giveaway from the News Of The World a British newspaper which was published between 1843 to closure in 2011. It was at one time the biggest selling English language newspaper in the world, and at closure still had one of the highest English language circulations.

NORTH EASTERN RAILWAY

Pictured below is an assembled cardboard lunch box produced by the North Eastern Railway.

North Eastern was a British Railroad Company serving the North East of England out of London. This box was likely used in the 1930's.

NECTAR TEA

Enamel tin sign advertising Nectar Tea with the slogan "The Cup that Cheers". Nectar Tea is a brand name owned by The Great Atlantic & Pacific Tea Company", the company is now known as A & P. During the 1930's A & P was the worlds largest retailer having over 16,000 stores. This sign showing a Willow pattern cup and saucer was most likely produced in the late 1940's/early 1950's.

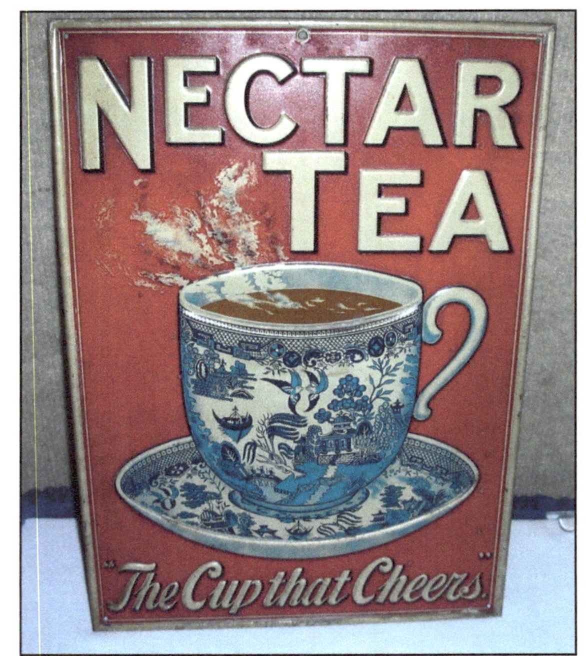

THE NEW YORKER

The New Yorker, a magazine printed out of New York over the years has used variations of the Willow pattern to illustrate the front cover of it's magazine.

14th November 1942

1st December 1957

7th January 1980

23rd July 1990

OUTWOOD WORKING MENS CLUB

Outwood Working Mens Club is a social members club that has a cooperative membership. The club is located in the Yorkshire town of Wakefield, England. Pictured below is a cup with the Parrott Pattern together with the club name and "CHILDRENS TREAT 1928". As the club is a cooperative they would have held events for member's children and in 1928 would have most likely given this cup to children as a gift.

THE OZARK MOUNTAIN DAREDEVILS "TOMD"

"TOMD" a popular band from the USA state of Missouri used the Willow pattern as a background to promote their second album (on vinyl record) titled "It'll Shine When it Shines" in 1973. The album was a top 5 world-wide hit. TOMD have produced 8 albums and have sold over 2 million. The band still plays concerts, with their music being described as a mix of Country, Appalchia, The South, and Rock & Roll. Inset left a lapel badge.

PEDRO DOMECQ

Pedro Domecq is a long established Spanish producer of sherry that during the 1960's and 1970's had a prominent market share of it's product in the UK. During those years, a glass of sherry was a popular drink both at home and at British Pubs. This tip tray is very similar to the ones produced by Schweppes.

PETER DAWSON'S SCOTCH WHISKY

PD Scotch was established in Scotland by Peter Dawson in 1896, but was taken over in 1898 by another manufacturer. The name of Peter Dawson remains today. These ashtrays were most likely produced in the 1930's.

PRICE'S WILLOW PATTERN CANDLES

Boxed pair of candles decorated with the Willow pattern. The candles are made by "Price's" and were produced in the 1930's.

R PILKINGTON GRAPES INN

Willow pattern vegetable dish which has on the centre of it "R Pilkington Grapes Inn". My research indicates that this piece was most likely made in England in the mid 1800's, but has revealed little as to who had this piece made for them. That said, there are several English pubs who have the name Grapes Inn, many of which are in the county of Yorkshire. In particular there is one pub in the Yorkshire city of Sheffield which is where I think this piece originates from.

PRIORY GREEN LABEL

Pictured right is a Tea Caddy which has on it a variation of the Willow pattern. The tin which would have contained 1 lb. of "Priory Green Label" tea was produced by Ellis & Manton of Wellington, New Zealand. During the first half of the 1900's Ellis & Manton were importers and distributors of numerous products. This tin was most likely produced between 1900 and 1915.

PUNCH ALMANACK

The Punch magazine was a weekly British publication which was established in 1841. It was a magazine known for it's humour and satire. The magazine was a British institution, but after the 1940's when it's circulation peaked at 184,000, it then went into a long period of decline, closing in 1992. It did reopen in 1996, but closed again in 2002 with only 6,000 subscribers. Pictured here is the front cover of the 1945 Punch Almanack where the Willow pattern has been adapted to portray the end of World War 2.

RINGTONS

Ringtons are still today a family owned business which operates from the city of Newcastle in England. The business was established in 1907 by Samuel Smith and sells tea by home delivery and more recently online. Over the years they have used Willow pattern teapots and caddies to support their sales.

ROCKFORD OATS

Pictured below is a breakfast bowl which has a variation of the Willow pattern in green on both the inside and outside of the bowl. The advertising effect of this piece is not directly visible until one looks at the base of the product, there the words 'Eat Rockford Oats" can be seen.

ROTERIA

Restaurant ware plate styled with the Willow pattern in brown. The plate has the marking "Roteria" which is probably the name of the restaurant which had this plate made. This plate was found in the USA.

RUPERT THE BEAR

Pictured right is the front cover of the 1954 children's annual Rupert, better known as Rupert the Bear. These annuals are produced by the Daily Express a daily British newspaper who ran a continuing children's feature story about Rupert and his friends. The annuals which come out just before Christmas have a collection of stories and puzzles in them. In 1954 the annual contained "Rupert's Willow Pattern Puzzle" which is pictured below. In this picture Rupert's friend Pong Ping is telling him about the legend of the Willow pattern. Rupert and the readers have to work out the legend by completing the missing words in a puzzle represented by pictures. Good luck with your efforts to work it out.

ROYAL CHINA

Advertisements for Royal China from the Crockery & Glass Journal, June 1949. The advertisements promote Royal China for promotional items and that they will be at the New York Show being held at the Hotel New Yorker.

SAINSBURYS

Sainsbury's are a national chain of food supermarkets in Britain. Pictured here is a Tea Caddy made of wood which they have used to package Earl Grey Tea Bags. The caddy measures 15 cm/6 inches on each side and is of recent production, circa 2006.

CATEDRAL DE SALTILLO

Souvenir plate of Catedral De Saltillo, a Cathedral located in the north of Mexico. Built between 1745 and 1800 during the Spanish colonial influence, Saltillo's cathedral, has one of Mexico's finest Churrigueresque facades, with columns of elaborately carved pale-gray stone. The central dome features carvings of Quetzalcóatl, the Aztec rain god.

SANDY MCNAB

Unmarked ashtray which was made in England and advertises Sandy Macnab Old Liqueur Scotch Whisky. This piece was most likely produced in the 1950's and used to advertise the liqueur whisky in British pubs.

SANDY MACDONALD

Unmarked ashtray which was made in England and advertises Sandy MacDonald Scotch Whisky. This piece was most likely produced in the 1930's and used to advertise the whisky in British pubs.

SAN FRANCISCO SOUVENIR 1

Here a Willow pattern ashtray of Japanese manufacture has been made into a tourist souvenir promoting San Francisco and the Golden Gate Bridge.

SAN FRANCISCO SOUVENIR 2

Souvenir plate which has for it's feature a depiction of San Francisco's China Town. Surrounding the central feature is a traditional border design seen on many blue Willow pattern plates. Note this patterned border is for reference very similar to that seen on the Cape Cod plate listed earlier in this book.

SNELLING'S

Small Willow pattern dish from the late 1890's which is marked "Snellings Potted Beef" along with the address "Rampant Horse St Norwich", a town in England. John Snelling operated a number of food and beverage businesses from his Rampant Horse Street premises during the 1890's.

SHERWOOD INN

Pictured here is a mug with the Willow pattern with the words "Sherwood Inn". The mug comes from England, the name Sherwood Inn is a popular British Pub name. Sherwood is the name of the forest which was home to the legendary Robin Hood, Friar Tuck, Little John and Maid Marion.

ST MARY'S MISSON CHURCH

St Mary's Mission Church was built in 1872 and closed in 1924. It was located in Baildon Green, a North Yorkshire village in England. This plate has the name of the church and village along with the year 1884. Most of the time the church was used as a school. This plate is typical of many issued by church schools during the 1800's.

SCHWEPPES TIP TRAYS

Schweppes was and still is a popular light drinks beverage company which was founded in England. The company in recent times has merged with chocolate and confectionary company Cadbury (also from England and in their own right have produced Willow advertising). Schweppes over the years have produced a variety of tip trays and water jugs, which have been mostly made in England, though some have been made in France.

SCHWEPPES TIP TRAYS

While I have been able to show seventeen tip trays, there are a few more in circulation. Over the years I have seen a "Table Water" and a "Sparkling Water". As these pieces are also keenly sought by brewiana collectors, I have seen some top prices paid for them. Also note that some of the tip trays have been produced in different colours.

SCHWEPPES JUGS

The jugs below which would have been used by British pubs and hotels were most likely produced in the 1930s. The jugs containing water would have been placed on bars where patrons could use them.

SCHWEPPES ASHTRAYS

Below are three ashtrays which in relative terms are quite modern and were probably produced in the 1980's for use in British pubs and hotels. These ashtrays are heavy ceramic pieces.

A PRESENT FROM SOUTHPORT

Pictured right is a cup which on the outside of the cup has a traditional Willow pattern. Inside the cup are the words "A Present From Southport"

Southport is a seaside town in the Northwest of England and this piece which is unmarked would of most likely have been made in the 1930's.

STAR BEERS

A tip tray and water jug advertising Star Beer "IPA". The IPA meaning Indian Pale Ale a bottled style of beer originating from England, a beer sometimes favored by the writer. These pieces which are made in England were most likely produced during the 1960's.

STANDISH LODGE

Standish Lodge is a Masonic Club in the town of Standish, Lancashire, England. This masonic lodge received it's number "4955" in 1894 and my guess would be that this cup was made to mark this occasion. The age and pattern on this piece are consistent with this year.

RICHARD STANWAY

Small Willow pattern medallion with the words "Richard Stanway Newcastle Staffs" In 1881 Richard S Stanway founded Enderley Mills in Newcastle, Staffordshire, England.

The Mill specialised in the manufacture of uniforms. At the time of Stanway's ownership, the Mill was viewed as a model one by the Government Inspector, as it included a surgery, crèche, reading room, and savings bank. After Stanway's bankruptcy in 1884, the business continued with new owners. This piece would have been used as a tailor's tag between 1881 and 1884.

STRINGYBACH

Stringybach were a musical quartet from Western Australia who played as a group between 1981 and 1990. Their instrumental music features the use of mandolins and guitars on which they played a repertoire of music ranging from classical themes to current day contemporary.

Pictured here is their album release "Weeping Willow" which uses Willow pattern on the cover of the CD. Additionally they have used the Willow pattern on the inside cover of the CD as a background to the index listing of music track titles, and on the CD itself.

SWAN HILL FOLK MUSEUM

Pictured here is a commemorative plate issued by Swan Hill Folk Museum to celebrate the visit of Queen Elizabeth II, April 1970. Swan Hill is a town in rural Victoria, Australia through which the Murray river flows. The plate has all of the Willow pattern features, but the pagodas have been replaced with Australian country houses, the boat is now a (Murray River) paddle steamer, and the people on the bridge have a sheep between them.

FULLER & SWATLAND

Fuller & Swatland Limited were an English company who had establishments in the British towns of Hastings and St. Leonards. As a company they were grocers, wine and beer merchants. Pictured below is a paper package which would have contained a 1/2 lb. of tea which they sold as "Empire Tea". This item was most likely produced in the 1920's and 1930's. The company closed in May 1948.

TEA MASTERS CEYLON

Packet of 25 "Raspberry" tea bags produced by Sri Lankan company Tea Masters Ceylon. This tea was produced for the North American market during the 1990's and was imported by Canadian importer Nick Kray. The tea is described as "Blue Willow" and the box has a cup and saucer in the Willow pattern to match this.

TEA TOWELS

Every Willow collector probably has a tea towel with the Willow pattern on it as they are plentiful and come in a variety of colours. Here are some tea towels which also have some advertising on them as well. The towel with "Tweed Heads" is from Australia and the other with "Save The Children" is a British Charity.

TELECOM

Rex and Molly featured for Telecom New Zealand in several of their advertisements. In this scene Molly is telling their owner that they've broken her (Willow) dinner plate service. This scene also appeared as a TV commercial where more Willow could be seen.

TENNENT'S

Tennent's Lager Beer is Scotland's most popular lager beer and was first produced in 1885. The company is based in Glasgow, Scotland. These tip trays similar to the Schweppes tip trays were most likely made in the 1920's for use in British pubs and hotels.

TEVNA TEA

Pictured below is a tea caddy which on the base is marked "Thomas & Evans Celebrated Tevna Tea". This piece was most likely produced in the 1920's. The business Thomas & Evans was founded in 1883 by William Evans with financial assistance from William Thomas. A condition of that assistance was that the business, a grocery store be called Thomas & Evans. William Evans soon established a chain of grocery stores in South Wales. Though these stores were a mainstay of his business, William Evans is better remembered for producing soft drinks under the Corona name which he did from 1887. William Evans died in 1934 at the age of 70 and whilst his business continued, it was sold in 1940.

TETLEY TEA

Found in Australia, Tetley used a Willow pattern teaset on their teabag packaging. They used this packaging for a few years around 2002.

TIFFANY & CO

Pictured below Coalport blue Willow pattern china advertisement in 1975 by Tiffany & Co.

TWININGS

Pictured right is a "Ginger Jar" which serves as a tea caddy for Twinings. The maker of this piece is Mason's of England, details of which are noted on the base. This piece was most likely made in the 1930's and came in several colours. The Mason's mark on this piece was used between 1891 and 1990.

Twinings is a world famous company which blends and sells tea. The business was established in 1706 by Thomas Twining in London and today the business blends 200 types of tea and operates in over 100 countries. The Twinings logo is the oldest in existence.

UNDERGROUND LONDON

The original artwork for this poster is held at the London Transport Museum Covent Garden, England. The picture depicts a London Underground Train travelling through the Willow Pattern.

USHERS SCOTCH WHISKY

Ashtray made for Usher's Scotch Whisky. Ushers is a popular Scotch Whisky distilled in Scotland and this ashtray was probably made in the 1920's.

VRAGG

Made in the 1890's this small Dutch advertising piece made in Maastricht has the Dutch words "Vraag B v/d Glansstijfsel" which translates to "Buy B v/d Linen Starch". B v/d is an abbreviation of the company name "B van der Sluys". Piece measures 11 cm/4 inches across.

VAN NELLLE

Van Nelle was a Dutch company based in the city of Rotterdam and produced tea, coffee and tobacco from the 1930's until they ceased production in the early 1990's. This small jug which appears to be of Japanese manufacture has the Van Nelle name at its base. The jug would have most likely been a promotional item being associated with their tea and coffee products.

VICTORY LOZENGES

These tins contained Victory V Lozenges and are decorated with the Willow pattern. The tins in height are 30 cm/12 inches. The lozenges were first made by Thomas Fryer in England in 1864, he was inspired by Horatio Nelson and his British Royal Navy Ship "Victory". As a palliative for the common cold, the lozenges contained chlorodyne a mix of chloroform and cannabis which proved to be very popular. These tins were probably made around the 1920's when the lozenges were available globally. Nowadays since the lozenges no longer contain chlorodyne (narcotics) sales are limited to confectionary shops.

THE VENTURE BASINGSTOKE

Small ashtray made for "The Venture" a British Pub in Basingstoke. The phone number on the ashtray indicates that this piece was probably made in the 1940's. As for "The Venture", my research has found that the Pub is no longer in existence, replaced by a road roundabout known as the Venture Roundabout.

WILLOW PATTERN POLKA

Piano solo sheet music written in 1892 by Joseph J Tarrant and published by W.H . Broome of London.

WIGLEYS BREAD

Pictured here is a Willow pattern plate which centered on it is "Eat Wigleys Bread". At the time of writing this book, the writer has not been able to source any information about Wigleys.

W.D. & H.O. WILLS

In 1895 Wills were one of the first British Tobacco Companies to insert collectable cards with their products. Pictured here is a card showing the Willow pattern, on the reverse of this card is the story of the Willow legend, this card is part of a set of 50, produced in the 1930's.

WHITTARD OF CHELSEA

Whittard of Chelsea, London are merchandisers of fine tea and coffee. They were established in 1886 and are still trading today. Pictured here is a tea caddy, with a teapot showing the Willow pattern that they have used to package their Yunnan leaf tea. A review of their catalogue which is available on their website indicates that they often use teapots with the Willow pattern to market their tea products.

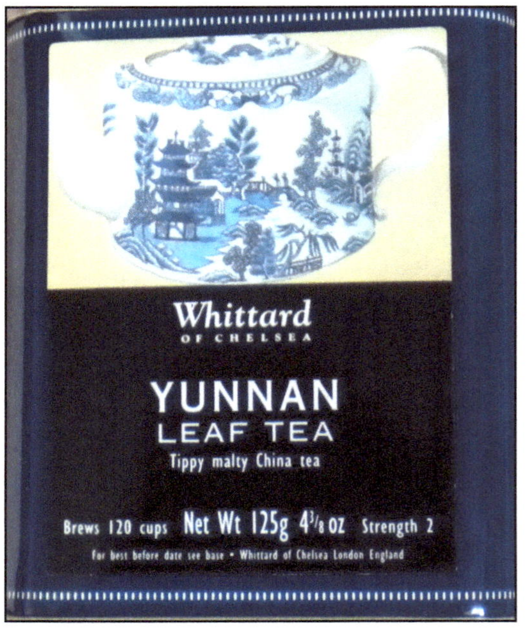

YORKSHIRE RELISH

Goodall, Backhouse "Goodalls" from the county of Yorkshire in England the makers of Yorkshire Relish were established in 1837 and produced Yorkshire Relish until 1960. Goodalls used the Willow pattern plate as a centre piece on their relish bottles and in their advertising. They produced two types of relish, thick or thin. In simple terms, the thick was like a barbeque plum sauce and the thin, like a Worcestershire sauce. The writer also has a relish bottle which in the glass of the base has the Willow pattern impressed in it. Pictured below are tip trays, a playing card and on the following page, paper advertisements.

YORKSHIRE RELISH

Above an advertisement from 1899, to the right 1929.

POSTCARD YORK

Below is a picture postcard in which the aspects of the Willow pattern have been changed to represent the historical and tourist sights of the city of York in England. My estimate is that this card would have been printed in the 1920's to 1930's.

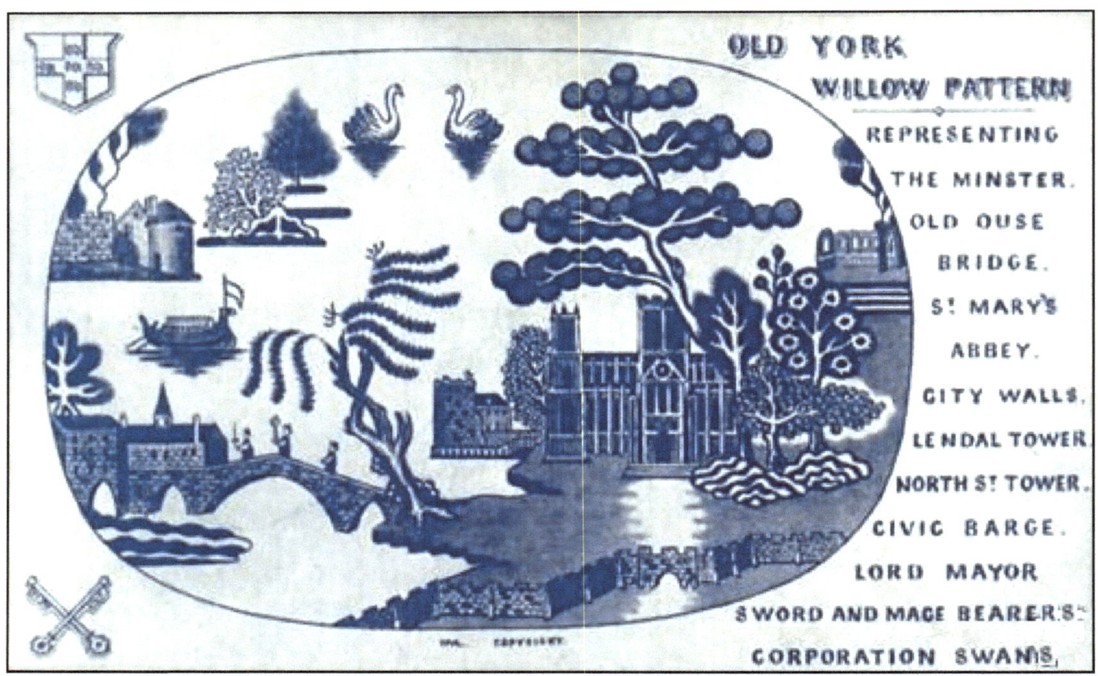

ADVERTISING A TO Z
FEATURING THE
BLUE WILLOW PATTERN

After being encouraged many times to do so, author Hugh Sykes has written this book which shows how the Blue Willow Pattern has been used to advertise and promote various products and services across the world.

Containing over 250 pictures showing how the pattern has been used, the book also provides historical and background information on each piece.

In this book you will see that many businesses have come and gone, one thing for sure though is that the legend of the Blue Willow Pattern remains strong and will continue to be used to advertise products for many years.

A Helsa Morgan Book

ISBN 978-0-473-24374-6